# My First Book About Dolphins

## Amazing Animals Books
## Children's Picture Books

By Molly Davidson

Mendon Cottage Books

*JD-Biz Publishing*

**Read More Amazing Animal Books**

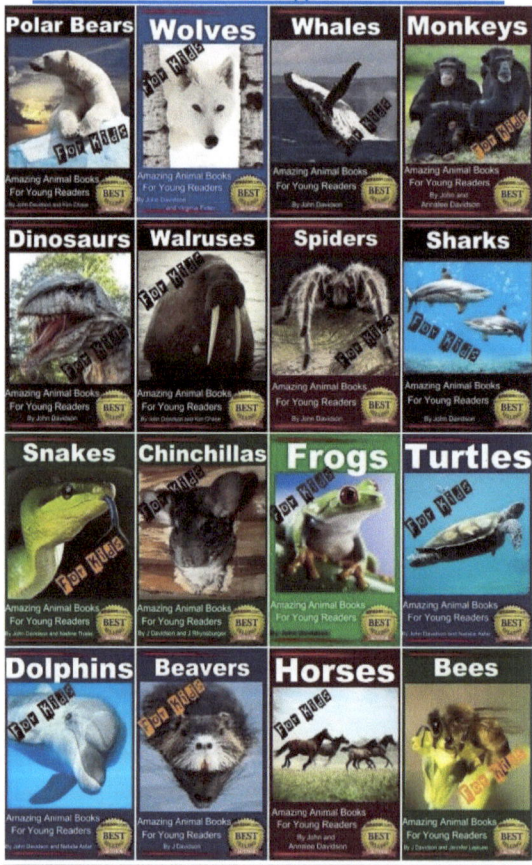

**Purchase at Amazon.com**

**Download Free Books!**
**http://MendonCottageBooks.com**

# Table of Contents

# 1. Introduction to Dolphins

Dolphins are well known to be friendly and calm, but they LOVE to play.

© anilah - Fotolia.com

## 2. Facts about Dolphins

Dolphins can stay 15 minutes under water, but they cannot breathe under the water.

All dolphins have a different color, most are a type of gray.

# 3. What Do You Know About Dolphins

Dolphins are water mammals. Mammals mean that they drink milk from their mother.

They live in the sea and deep warm waters because dolphins can't live in cold waters.

Some dolphins, like these, live in rivers!

## 4. Types of Dolphins

The babies are called calves, the moms are called dolphins, and the boys are called bulls.

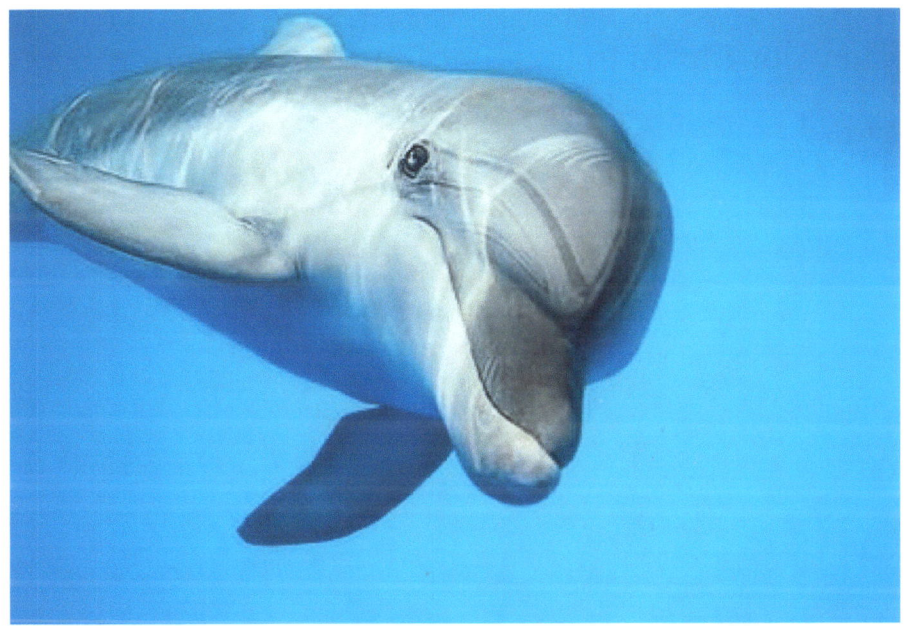

© Andriy Bezuglov - Fotolia.com

Dolphins  talk through making sounds and whistles.

## 5. Baby Dolphins (Calves)

Calves eat their mother's milk for 2 years after being born.

They don't learn to hunt until they are about 6 years old.

© Lynne Nicholson - Fotolia.com

## 6. Why Dolphins Live in Water

Dolphins eat fish, and fish can only be found in the water, so dolphins live near their food.

© Colette - Fotolia.com

**Also, Dolphins are born with fins, not legs. Fins are used for swimming in water.**

# 7. Dolphins Traveling in Water

Dolphins like warm water, so when winter comes, they travel together in groups, to warmer places in the ocean.

© Angelo Giampiccolo - Fotolia.com

## 8. How Dolphins Breathe

There is a hole on top of its head where they blow water out and when they dive, they close their hole up so water doesn't come in.

© Kerri McClellan - Fotolia.com

## 9. Dolphins Can Smell and See

© Gennadiy Poznyakov - Fotolia.com

Dolphins have very good eyesight. They need this to protect themselves from predators in the sea water.

Even though dolphins can smell and see, they cannot taste!

## 10. What Dolphins Eat

Dolphins work as a team to gather lots of fish together, then they can all eat at the same time.

© Matthew Cole - Fotolia.com

## 11. Dolphins Live With Family

Dolphins travel in family groups called a school.

Up to 1,000 dolphins can be in a group, if there is enough food in one area for everyone.

Groups usually have about 12 dolphins.

# 12. Dolphins Can Be Your Friends

© Maxim Larin - Fotolia.com

Yes, dolphins can be your friend, they will never hurt you, as long as you are friendly with them.

## 13. Dolphins Play in Water

Dolphins are great swimmers and enjoy jumping out of the water and doing flips in the air.

© Tatjana Keisa - Fotolia.com

Surfers have reported seeing dolphins body surfing in the waves next to them.

## 14. Dolphins Sleep Too

Dolphins sleep by resting one half of their brain at a time.

This means that one side of the dolphin's brain is awake while the other is in a deep sleep.

## 15. What Harms Dolphins?

© Andrey Armyagov - Fotolia.com

Cold weather, dolphins only like warm water, this is why they always swim to where it is warm.

Dolphins can get caught in fishing nets and die.

Sharks will sometimes kill dolphins for food.

# 16. People Can Harm Dolphins

People often visit their habitat and leave litter there.

If a dolphin eats garbage it could get sick, and maybe even die.

# 17. Rare Dolphins

© tazzymon - Fotolia.com

Hectore Dolphins: They are very rare, and are the smallest dolphins.

River Dolphins : Only 4 kinds of dolphins being able to live in rivers

Our books are available at

1. Amazon.com
2. Barnes and Noble
3. Itunes
4. Kobo
5. Smashwords
6. Google Play Books

**Download Free Books!**
**http://MendonCottageBooks.com**

# Publisher

JD-Biz Corp

P O Box 374

Mendon, Utah 84325

http://www.jd-biz.com/